PRESENTED TO:

_____

PRESENTED BY:

_____

DATE:

_____

Time to Shine, Graduate!

Graduate!

Make the Moments Count

WHITE STONE BOOKS

LAKELAND, FLORIDA

Time to Shine, Graduate!
—Make the Moments Count
ISBN: 1-59379-036-8
Copyright © 2005 White Stone Books
P.O. Box 2835
Lakeland, Florida 33806

10 09 08 07 06 05   10 9 8 7 6 5 4 3 2 1

Scripture reference credit lines are located on page 95.

Introduction

You are finally about to embark on a brand new journey toward your future. You will be making your own decisions. You know you're ready. You have dreams to pursue. You want to make a difference in the world.

Are you looking for some inside information, now that you've graduated?

Time to Shine Graduate is your handy little reference guide, filled with inspiring quotes, uplifting verses, and motivating challenges for personal growth. You'll also find quick tips on a full-range of light-hearted and serious topics; not to mention savvy advice on how to navigate the exhilarating and winding road of independence.

With the confidence that comes from your significant accomplishment—now really is your time to shine!

Table of Contents

Time to Shine, Graduate!

Make the Moments Count

Keep Your Eyes on the Goal

"BE THE BEST YOU CAN BE AND KEEP
YOUR EYES ON THE GOAL."

—HENRY "HANK" AARON—
BOSTON BRAVES BASEBALL TEAM & NATIONAL BASEBALL HALL OF FAME

Find out what you love, what comes
naturally, and write it down.
Then pursue it as long and as
hard as you can. Build your dream
around it, and never give up.

Trust God from the bottom of your heart;
don't try to figure out everything on your own.
Listen for GOD's voice in everything you do, everywhere
you go; he's the one who will keep you on track.

PROVERBS 3:5-6 MSG

Finding Good Role Models

Learn from the wisdom of others who have gone before you. By reaching outside of your sphere of friends, you give yourself a safe environment to share your thoughts and ask questions. Mentors can greatly increase your life's learning curve and give you an edge in business, relationships, and the challenges of life.

▸ **CONNECT WITH A TEACHER:**

Look for a teacher who has qualities you admire. Communicate and ask questions. It's a great way to grow and develop a possible friendship in a learning environment.

▸ **CONNECT WITH A SUPERVISOR:**

Look for a leader in a work environment who casts vision and respects others. Offer to take him or her to lunch and "pick their brain" on how they became successful.

▸ **CONNECT WITH A CHURCH ELDER:**

Look for an elder or senior member in your local church who operates with grace and compassion. Approach them about meeting you on a regular basis and mentoring you in the things of life. It's an opportunity to glean from their wisdom and to form a meaningful new friendship.

▸ **CONNECT WITH STUDENTS WHO MAKE THINGS HAPPEN:**

Look for students who are involved in campus life and making a difference. Hook up with some of their projects and get to know them. Discover how they lead others and how they support their leadership.

▸ **CONNECT WITH A FAMILY MEMBER:**

An aunt, uncle, or grandparent can be an excellent source of support especially when you are away from home.

▸ **CONNECT WITH A FAMILY FRIEND:**

Look for someone who is good in business, full of integrity, and dependable. Someone who has been involved in your family for years. Bounce things off of them and ask them for their advice.

"LOVE YOURSELF FIRST AND EVERYTHING
ELSE FALLS INTO LINE."

—LUCILLE BALL—
EMMY AWARD WINNING ACTRESS

As you are pursuing your dream,
be sure to incorporate laughter
into your journey. Make someone
laugh today. It will do you both
good and it just might bring
you closer to your dream.

All the days of the oppressed are wretched,
but the cheerful heart has a continual feast.

PROVERBS 15:15

Work and Have Fun

"RESPECT YOURSELF AS WELL AS OTHERS;
MAKE COMMITMENTS, NOT EXCUSES,
AND MAKE EVERY DAY A FUN DAY."

—WALLY AMOS—
SUCCESSFUL BUSINESSMAN AND FOUNDER OF FAMOUS AMOS COOKIES

If we think positive and take
action, we can have fun and
follow our sweet dreams to success.
Think of something fun you can
do today that is related to your
fulfilling your dream and do it.

*Whatever you do, work at it with all your heart,
as working for the Lord.*

COLOSSIANS 3:23

MAKE THE MOMENTS COUNT.

On a Date Without Much Money

It's not about how much money you spend but about the quality of time you spend together. And, it's not about what you're doing, it's about who you're doing it with. Invest your time with the right person and have fun just being together.

▸ GO TO A COFFEE HOUSE AND PLAY A BOARD GAME

▸ HIKE IN A LOCAL WILDLIFE PARK

▸ GO BIKE RIDING. IF YOU DON'T HAVE A BIKE, YOU CAN RENT BIKES IN MOST CITIES.

▸ EAT CHINESE TAKE-OUT IN THE PARK

- ▶ ATTEND CAMPUS EVENTS TOGETHER

- ▶ TAKE AN EVENING WALK IN A PARK

- ▶ GO FOR ICE CREAM CONES AND READ THE NEWSPAPER COMICS

- ▶ BUY A BOX OF CHEESE CRACKERS AND FEED THE DUCKS AT A LOCAL POND

- ▶ GO FOR AN EVENING DRIVE, PLAY A GOOD CD, AND EXPLORE A NEW PART OF TOWN

- ▶ HAVE A PICNIC ON CAMPUS

- ▶ GO TO THE DOLLAR THEATER FOR A GOOD SHOW

- ▶ GO TO SUNDAY OPEN HOUSES AROUND TOWN AND EXPLORE

Multitasking

"I'M HAVING SO MUCH FUN. IT'S AMAZING
HOW ALL THESE PARTS OF MY LIFE OVERLAP."

—RHONDA BAKER—
EPISCOPAL REVEREND, MS SURVIVOR, AND FIREFIGHTER

Are you multitasking but stressed out? It is important to recognize your limitations, but try **setting your priorities** and combining your passions. It may help you realize your dreams in a way that is more enjoyable, peaceful, and fulfilling.

May our Lord Jesus Christ himself and God our Father, who loved us and by his grace gave us eternal encouragement and good hope, encourage your hearts and strengthen you in every good deed and word.

2 THESSALONIANS 2:16-17

Reaching Out

"I MAY BE COMPELLED TO FACE DANGER,
BUT NEVER FEAR IT...."

—CLARA BARTON—
CIVIL WAR NURSE AND PRESIDENT OF
THE NATIONAL SOCIETY OF THE RED CROSS

It takes courage and trust to stop and reach out to others while pursing your own dream, but whatever good you do for others, God will do for you.

With good will doing service, as to the Lord, and not to men: knowing that whatsoever good thing any man doeth, the same shall he receive of the Lord, whether he be bond or free.

EPHESIANS 6:7-8 KJV

New Roommates

Roommates can be a blessing and a challenge. Get yourself off to the right start by setting some reasonable boundaries.

▸ RESPECT:

Every person deserves to have the respect of others. That means treating your roommate and their property with honor and consideration.

▸ QUIET TIME:

Agree on a time in the evening when the music, television, and lights are turned down. Get some headphones if you need to. That way you both can have your own space and/or get some sleep.

▸ MAY I BORROW THIS?:

Before you borrow—ASK! If you use it up—replace it.

▶ Keep It Neat and Tidy:

If it's a mess, close the door! If you don't share your roommate's cleaning habits, have a place where you can stash your mess. No one wants to look at your dirt!

▶ Lights Out:

So your roommate snores or maybe you do. Invest in a set of earplugs. They don't cost much and they work wonders.

▶ Visitors:

Be considerate about bringing people over to your room. Check with your roommate to make sure it works for them. When possible, meet your friends elsewhere.

Be an Overcomer

"I SHALL SEIZE FATE BY THE THROAT; IT SHALL
CERTAINLY NOT BEND AND CRUSH ME...."

—BEETHOVEN—
GIFTED COMPOSER AND MUSICAL GENIUS, DESPITE BEING DEAF

Has adversity come against you that would try to defeat you and steal your dream? Perhaps through the words of others or even some failure on your part? **Never give up!** The Greater One lives in you, and through Him, you will overcome.

*[Jesus said,] "In the world you will have tribulation;
but be of good cheer, I have overcome the world."*

JOHN 16:33 NKJV

"YOUNG PEOPLE, GIVEN ENOUGH SCHOOLING
AND USING THE BRAINS THEY WERE BORN WITH,
CAN RISE ABOVE THEMSELVES AS FAR AS THEY
WANT TO GO, THE SKY THE LIMIT."

—CARRINE GAFKJEN BERG—
NORWEGIAN IMMIGRANT AND SUCCESSFUL FEMALE LANDOWNER
OF 320 ACRES FROM THE EARLY 1900'S

Are you willing to count the cost and **follow through** until your dream is realized? Write down the sacrifices and commitments you know you will have to make, along with your decision to make them. Post it somewhere that you will see it and be reminded often.

The sleep of a laborer is sweet,
whether he eats little or much.

ECCLESIASTES 5:12

MAKE THE MOMENTS COUNT.

Great Ways to
Save Cash!

*When you're on your own every dollar counts.
Here's a few ways to save yourself a little
money and make your dollars stretch.*

▶ **COFFEE:**

Hanging out at the coffee house is fun, but watch the
gourmet coffees. They can add up fast. Limit yourself to
no more than one a day. If you're going to study or get
on the web while you're there, get a "bottomless cup."

▶ **CELL PHONE:**

The minutes can disappear on some cell phone plans.
Try to get a plan with unlimited local calls or get on a
plan where you can share with your friends and family
so your calls are free. If all else fails, limit your calls to
the unlimited calling hours.

▶ FOOD:

Eating out can whittle away your spending money. Try to have some meals at home or if you are in school—hit the cafeteria. If you do go out, order from the specials section, and back off ordering sodas, drink water instead. It's better for you and costs a lot less.

▶ CLOTHES:

It's okay to get quality clothes as long as the styles and colors are classic so that they won't be out of style next season. For those trendy buys—search for inexpensive clothes or designer second-hand stores. Shop a few discount stores instead of spending all your time at the mall.

▶ MUSIC:

You gotta have it! Get your MP3 player and download your favorite songs off the web instead of buying the whole CD.

Think Positive

"Don't quack like a duck, soar like an eagle. Ducks complain and quack about what is not right. Eagles soar above the fray."

—Kenneth Blanchard—
Popular Motivational Speaker and Bestselling Author of
Seventeen Titles including *The One Minute Manager*

Accentuate the positive.
Diminish the negative.
Imagine what you most want to be,
make it real in your mind, and
pursue it with all your heart.

Be very careful, then, how you live—not as unwise but as wise, making the most of every opportunity.

Ephesians 5:15-16

Living for Something
Greater Than Yourself

"THE GREATNESS OF A MAN'S POWER IS THE
MEASURE OF HIS SURRENDER."

—WILLIAM BOOTH—
FOUNDER OF THE SALVATION ARMY

Are you willing to **dedicate yourself** to the greater good? What is your mission statement? Write it down and let it act as a guide to keep you on course.

We who are strong ought to bear with the failings of the weak and not to please ourselves. Each of us should please his neighbor for his good, to build him up.

ROMANS 15:1-2

Get Rid of That Stress!

Stress is a very real part of life. Whether your day is taking you to the workplace or another class, try some of these helpful tips when the pressure seems to be overwhelming.

▶ **GET EXTRA REST:**

Make sure to get plenty of sleep. Not only will this help relieve stress, but it will also help you to avoid that nasty cold that is going around!

▶ **BE ON TIME:**

It can be very stressful when you are in a constant scramble to catch up with the day. If necessary, set your clock a couple of minutes ahead of the actual time to give yourself a cushion.

- ### Kick Your Shoes Off:

  Take a break and relax for a minute. Calm your mind and body down. Meditate on a great scripture and remember that nothing is worth losing your peace over.

- ### Play Some Soft Music:

  Classical or soft music can help revitalize and relax the mind, body, and spirit.

- ### Give Your Cares Over to God:

  It can be difficult to let go of everything and trust God, but remember that He can handle it much better than you! When you ask Him to help, He really does, but you have to ask.

Give of Yourself

"NO MAN CAN BECOME RICH WITHOUT
HIMSELF ENRICHING OTHERS."

—ANDREW CARNEGIE—
SCOTTISH IMMIGRANT, ENTREPRENEUR, OWNER OF
CARNEGIE STEEL COMPANY (A LEADER IN THE STEEL INDUSTRY),
AND BENEFACTOR FOR MANY LIBRARIES ESTABLISHED ACROSS AMERICA.

Ask several people you know what
their dreams are, then think of
some ways you can invest in the
advancement of those dreams.
Even if it is your time or simply
an encouraging word, contribute
something today.

*It is possible to give freely and become more wealthy,
but those who are stingy will lose everything.*

PROVERBS 11:24 NLT

Discover What Makes You Tick

"SOME SHIPS RIDE OUT THE STORM BEST IF THE
ENGINES ARE STOPPED AND THE VESSEL IS
PERMITTED TO SEEK ITS OWN POSITION."

—NATHANIEL BOWDITCH—
A LOVER OF MATHEMATICS, AT AGE 21 WROTE *THE NEW AMERICAN
PRACTICAL NAVIGATOR*, A BOOK STILL EXTENSIVELY USED BY THE
U.S. NAVY AND CONSIDERED TO BE THE "SEAMAN'S BIBLE."

What are your obligations and
responsibilities? While being
faithful to fulfill them, determine
to use your "free" time to invest in
the study of your dream. Even today,
do a search on the Internet and
see what nuggets you can find.

*Thy way is in the sea, and thy path in the great waters,
and thy footsteps are not known.*

PSALM 77:19 KJV

31

Hungry in a Pinch

*Keep these quick eats handy when you can't
get out. If you can bring in a small refrigerator,
you can keep cool snacks too! Tuck a microwave
in your room. They are very inexpensive
and can fit just about anywhere.*

▸ **ANYWHERE SNACKS:**

Raisins, Packaged Nuts (Sunflower Seeds, Pumpkin
Seeds, Soy Nuts, Almonds, Peanuts, Cashews, Pecans,
Black Walnuts), Bottled Water, Oranges or Apples, Trail
Mix, Snack Cereal Boxes, Breakfast Bars, Pop Tarts,
Dark Chocolate, Bananas, Yogurt Covered Raisins.

► **Cool Snacks:**

Juices, Bottled Coffee Drinks, Energy Drinks, Smoothies, Yogurt, Grapes, Cheese, Lunch Meats, Bagels and Cream Cheese, Carrots, Celery Sticks, and Ranch Dressing.

► **Microwave Snacks:**

Popcorn, Mac & Cheese, Rice Bowls, Ramen Noodles, S'mores, Instant Oatmeal, Nachos, Hot Dogs, Hot Chocolate, Tea.

Ask God for Wisdom

"DO THE COMMON THINGS OF LIFE
IN AN UNCOMMON WAY...."

—GEORGE WASHINGTON CARVER—
AFRICAN-AMERICAN AGRICULTURAL CHEMIST AND AGRONOMIST OF THE EARLY
1900S WHOSE RESEARCH OF PEANUTS, SWEET POTATOES, AND SOYBEANS
HELPED DEVELOP HUNDREDS OF PRODUCTS INCLUDING PAINT,
SALVES, FOODS, BUILDING MATERIALS, AND BABY FORMULA.

Are you **taking every opportunity** to learn new things? Choose one topic of great interest to you and determine to learn everything you can about it. Then ask God to add His wisdom to your knowledge and get ready for endless possibilities.

Then you will understand what is right and just and fair—every good path. For wisdom will enter your heart, and knowledge will be pleasant to your soul.

PROVERBS 2:9-10

Giving and Receiving

"NEARLY EVERY MOMENT OF EVERY DAY WE HAVE THE
OPPORTUNITY TO GIVE SOMETHING TO SOMEONE
ELSE—OUR TIME, OUR LOVE, OUR RESOURCES.
I HAVE ALWAYS FOUND MORE JOY IN GIVING WHEN
I DID NOT EXPECT ANYTHING IN RETURN."

—S. TRUETT CATHY—
FOUNDER OF THE BILLION-DOLLAR FRANCHISE CHICK-FIL-A

The act of giving to others when nothing is expected in return sows seeds of greatness into your future. It's the principle of sowing and reaping, giving and receiving. Doing great things tomorrow begins with a willingness to do small things today. Take a minute to reflect on your character. What kind of seeds have you sown?

*Remember this: Whoever sows sparingly
will also reap sparingly, and whoever sows
generously will also reap generously.*

2 CORINTHIANS 9:6

When You Get the Blues

▸ **GET ON THE PHONE:**

Call someone who always makes you laugh or is supportive in all you do.

▸ **TAKE A WALK:**

Soak up some sun. Sunshine can do wonders for the heart and exercise releases important endorphins in your system.

▸ **READ THE COMICS:**

Get your mind off of your cares. The Scriptures say that laughter is good like a medicine.

▸ **PLAY UPBEAT MUSIC:**

Music gets in your soul. Change your atmosphere with music that lifts your spirits.

▸ PULL A FUNNY PRANK:

Laugh with a friend over a funny prank.

▸ SCRIPTURE ENCOURAGEMENT:

Write out some encouraging Scriptures and put them where you can see them: Jeremiah 29:11, Isaiah 41:10, Psalm 37:4, Psalm 139, John 14:1.

▸ WATCH A FUNNY MOVIE:

Don't put something on that will make you sad or tie you up with suspense. Put something on that will make you laugh!

> "MY MOTHER'S WORDS ALWAYS GAVE ME THE
> STRENGTH TO OVERCOME OBSTACLES."
>
> —BESSIE COLEMAN—
> A CHAMPION WHO WOULD NOT TAKE "NO"
> FOR AN ANSWER AND AGAINST AMAZING OBSTACLES
> BECAME THE FIRST BLACK WOMAN PILOT—1921

Take one step today
toward **overcoming an
obstacle** between you
and your life's dream.

*With your help I can advance against a troop;
with my God I can scale a wall.*

2 SAMUEL 22:30

Forgiveness

"LET THE MORNING BRING ME WORD OF YOUR
UNFAILING LOVE, FOR I HAVE PUT MY TRUST
IN YOU. SHOW ME THE WAY I SHOULD GO,
FOR TO YOU I LIFT UP MY SOUL."

—KING DAVID—
THE SECOND KING OF ISRAEL KNOWN AS A "MAN AFTER GOD'S OWN HEART"

Is there **something** in your life
holding you back? If so, write
it down on a sheet of paper and
ask God for His forgiveness. Then
destroy the paper and thank Him for
His faithfulness and let it be a
turning point in your life.

*Create in me a pure heart, O God, and renew a
steadfast spirit within me. Do not cast me from
your presence or take your Holy Spirit from me.
Restore to me the joy of your salvation and
grant me a willing spirit, to sustain me.*

PSALM 51:10-12

Stay in Touch

Before you lose touch with the people you care about, do yourself a favor and stay connected. Even though your paths may be going a different way, the friendships you've made can last a lifetime with a little effort in communication.

▸ **INVEST IN AN ADDRESS BOOK:**

Use a palm pilot, laptop, or a nice ruled book.

▸ **SEND AN E-MAIL:**

It only takes a few seconds to E-mail a friend or send a crazy E-card. Make a distribution list for all your friends and send them frequent updates to what's happening in your life.

► **MAKE A CALL:**

Use your anytime minutes. They're free! Send a fun picture of yourself on your cell phone. Show your friends your new mustache or hair cut.

► **WRITE A LETTER:**

The post office is still in business, and it's still fun to send and receive letters. Write down a cool memory of time spent with your friend.

► **CALL YOUR MOTHER:**

Enough said!

► **SEND AN IM:**

You think you don't have time? Send a smiley face.

► **USE YOUR CALENDAR:**

Schedule birthday reminders to pop up on your screen.

Follow Your Gift

"IF YOU CAN DREAM IT, YOU CAN DO IT."

—WALT DISNEY—
AMERICAN MOTION-PICTURE AND TELEVISION PRODUCER, FOUNDER OF
THE DISNEY COMPANY, A FAMILY ENTERTAINMENT CORPORATION.

What do you enjoy? What is your passion? It may only be a hobby or pastime, but it could be your strongest talent. Follow that gifting. Search out what you enjoy most and develop it. It could be your destiny.

Delight yourself in the LORD and he will give you the desires of your heart.

PSALM 37:4

Within Your Power

"WE HAVE LEARNED THAT POWER IS A POSITIVE
FORCE IF IT IS USED FOR A POSITIVE PURPOSE."

—ELIZABETH DOLE—

U. S. SENATOR FROM NORTH CAROLINA, NATIONAL DIRECTOR OF
EDUCATION AND INFORMATION OF HOSPICE, FORMER SECRETARY OF
TRANSPORTATION, FORMER SECRETARY OF LABOR, FORMER PRESIDENT OF
THE AMERICAN RED CROSS, HUMANITARIAN, AND SUCCESSFUL CHRISTIAN
WOMAN WHO CONSISTENTLY CHAMPIONS THE RIGHTS OF OTHERS.

Think of one person or several
people in your sphere of influence
who could benefit from something
you are good at. Take one step in that
direction today and put your gifts and
talents to work to bless others.

*Do not withhold good from those who deserve it,
when it is in your power to act.*

PROVERBS 3:27

MAKE THE MOMENTS COUNT.

Creating Positive and Indulgent Self-Rewards

Life is to be enjoyed. It's easy to get burned out if you are constantly driving yourself to accomplish goals or please others. It's important to also invest in yourself. When you've finished a project or scored well on a test give yourself a reward.

▶ **CLOSE THE BOOKS:**

Light a few candles, put on some smooth jazz, and kick back.

▶ **TAKE IN A LIVE PERFORMANCE:**

Movies are great, but nothing is like a live performance. Enjoy a great evening with a friend.

▶ GET A MASSAGE:

A shoulder massage is inexpensive and relaxing or go for a full body massage for a real treat. Even a pedicure or manicure is a soothing experience.

▶ GO SHOPPING:

Even if cash is low, reward yourself with a small item at your favorite store.

▶ TAKE A WEEKEND GETAWAY:

Go camping with some friends. It doesn't cost much to sleep in a tent and enjoy a campfire.

▶ EAT A WHOLE CHEESECAKE:

Kidding...just eat one piece!

> "WHAT IS POSSIBLE FOR ME
> IS POSSIBLE FOR YOU."
>
> —FREDERICK DOUGLASS—
> DIGNITARY, AUTHOR, PUBLISHER, AND LIBERATED SLAVE

What chains try to keep you from achieving your dreams? Pinpoint your fears and meet them head on. Don't let anything hold you back from accomplishing what's already in your heart.

If the Son sets you free, you will be free indeed.

JOHN 8:36

Great Possibilities

"ADVENTURE IS WORTHWHILE IN ITSELF."

—AMELIA EARHART—
THE FIRST WOMAN AVIATOR TO CROSS THE ATLANTIC SOLO.

Go outside tonight and look up at the sky. As you contemplate the vastness of the universe and the greatness of our God who made it, imagine what great possibilities lie ahead for you. Define your dream.

Jesus looked at them and said, "With man this is impossible, but not with God; all things are possible with God."

MARK 10:27

The New Kid on the Block

So you're the new kid. The best way to make friends is to get involved.

▸ **JOIN A CAMPUS GROUP:**

Get online with your school and find out what groups are available. Find one that fits your style and join up.

▸ **CHECK OUT YOUR COMMUNITY CENTER:**

Communities have all kinds of groups. You can meet people with similar interests just by attending classes or small groups.

▶ Volunteer Your Time:

There are hundreds of programs that need volunteers. Nothing will bring joy to your life like giving to others—after school youth programs, senior citizen homes, Meals on Wheels, Habitat for Humanity, and many others.

▶ Join a Political Party:

You're old enough to vote; now let your voice be heard!

▶ Get Involved in a Local Church:

Attend a singles' group or a college and career class.

▶ Become Part of a Drama Team:

Develop a talent and skill with a group of friends.

▶ Get Involved in Missions:

It's a great opportunity to experience new cultures and travel abroad!

The Rewards of Your Work

"GENIUS IS 1 PERCENT INSPIRATION AND
99 PERCENT PERSPIRATION."

—THOMAS A. EDISON—
GIFTED GENIUS AND INVENTOR OF OVER 1,000 INVENTIONS
INCLUDING THE ELECTRIC LIGHT BULB, THE PHONOGRAPH,
AND THE FIRST ELECTRIC POWER STATION

Write up a plan for the better use
of your free time and how to
maximize the hours devoted to work.
Learn to minimize distractions and
keep your focus on the goal.
Achievement brings great satisfaction.

Many good things come from what a man says,
and the work of his hands rewards him.

PROVERBS 12:14 NIRV

Define Success

"ALL OF US OUGHT TO HAVE SOME KIND OF CAUSE,
SOME KIND OF PURPOSE IN OUR LIVES, THAT'S
BIGGER THAN OUR OWN INDIVIDUAL HOPES,
DREAMS, WANTS, AND DESIRES."

—JOE EHRMANN—
MINISTER, FOUNDER OF THE DOOR INNER-CITY COMMUNITY
CENTER AND MISSION BALTIMORE, DEFENSIVE COACH FOR
THE EAST BALTIMORE HIGH SCHOOL FOOTBALL TEAM, AND
RETIRED BALTIMORE COLT DEFENSIVE LINEMAN

Assess your own beliefs about success.
How do you define it? What will it
look like when you achieve it in your
own life? Throw out any false beliefs
about success and build on those that
are right and good. Commit to
being real in all your relationships.

*Do your best to present yourself to God as one
approved, a workman who does not need to be
ashamed and who correctly handles the word of truth.*

2 TIMOTHY 2:15

MAKE THE MOMENTS COUNT.

Great Books That Will Change Your Life

If you want to develop your character, increase in wisdom, and open your mind to new possibilities, then taking in a few good books is a must. Check out the ones below.

- ▸ *I DARE YOU*
  by William Danforth

- ▸ *THE GO GETTER*
  by Peter B. Kyne, Alan Axelrod

- ▸ *MERE CHRISTIANITY*
  by C. S. Lewis

- ▸ *CUSTOMERS FOR LIFE*
  by Carl Sewell, Paul B. Brown

- *OH, THE PLACES YOU'LL GO!*
  by Dr. Seuss

- *THE HOLY BIBLE:*
  Start with the *Book of John, The Psalms,* and
  The Book of Proverbs.

- *HOW TO WIN FRIENDS AND INFLUENCE PEOPLE*
  by Dale Carnegie

- *HOW TO LIVE 365 DAYS A YEAR*
  by John A. Schindler, M.D.

- *THE RICHEST MAN IN BABYLON*
  by George S. Clason

- *THE MAGIC OF THINKING BIG*
  by David Schwartz

- *SEE YOU AT THE TOP*
  by Zig Ziglar

Seek Wisdom

> "LOST TIME IS NEVER FOUND AGAIN."

—BENJAMIN FRANKLIN—

THE YOUNGEST OF 10 BOYS AND APPRENTICE FOR 9 YEARS AS A WRITER AND PRINTER, LATER TO REALIZE HIS DREAM BY BECOMING THE OWNER OF HIS OWN PRINTING PRESS AND WRITER OF THE *POOR RICHARD'S ALMANAC*, WHICH CONTAINED A CALENDAR, WEATHER FORECASTS, POEMS, AND WISE SAYINGS. HE BECAME A STATESMAN, DRAFTING THE FIRST AND THE SECOND CONTINENTAL CONGRESS AND HELPED DRAW UP THE CONSTITUTION OF THE UNITED STATES AS WELL AS INVENTING MANY USEFUL EVERYDAY ITEMS.

Write down the things that you have been told by your mentors. Keep a file and refer to it often when you need a moment of inspiration. From time to time, review your file and be encouraged.

I wisdom dwell with prudence, and find out knowledge of witty inventions.

PROVERBS 8:12 KJV

Motivated to Greatness

"THE WHOLE SECRET TO EDUCATION
IS MOTIVATION."

—JAMES GOODRICH, M.D.—
ONCE A MEDIOCRE HIGH SCHOOL STUDENT WITH A LOW SAT SCORE,
TODAY, A RENOWNED NEUROSURGEON AND THE DIRECTOR OF
PEDIATRIC NEUROSURGERY AT MONTEFIORE MEDICAL CENTER IN
NEW YORK CITY. ONE LIFE-CHANGING EXPERIENCE WATCHING A
VIETNAMESE SURGEON OPERATE ON A SOLDIER CHANGED HIS LIFE FOREVER!

Open your eyes to the things that happen around you each day, watch for those things that set your heart on fire! It's often the gift that God has put inside you. Let it motivate you to achieve greatness.

*Remember also your Creator in the
days of your youth..."*

ECCLESIASTES 12:1 AMP

55

MAKE THE
MOMENTS COUNT.

Dirty Laundry

(Your Personal Guide to the Washing Machine)

*The real thing. We've all got it and it has
to be done. If you follow a few basic steps,
your clothes will look better and last longer.*

▶ **SORT YOUR CLOTHES:**

Into whites, lights, darks, and colors. Wash whites and
lights in hot, darks in warm, and colors in cold. That
way the colors won't bleed all over your other clothes.

▶ **DON'T OVERLOAD YOUR WASHER:**

Your clothes just don't get as clean.

▶ **TO GET RID OF STAINS:**

Use a spray stain remover or spot treat with liquid
laundry detergent and a good scrub with an old

toothbrush before your clothes go in the washer.
Check your clothes when they come out and make
sure the stain is gone before you put it in the dryer.
Once a stain has been in the dryer cycle, you risk
setting the stain permanently.

- ## ONLY USE BLEACH FOR WHITES, TOWELS, AND SHEETS:

   It can fade colors and spot your darks. Use special
   bleach products for colors.

- ## IF YOU ARE WORRIED ABOUT SOMETHING SHRINKING:

   Do yourself a favor and hang it up to dry.

You Can Overcome Adversity

"Ordinary people can make a huge difference."

—Tricia Goyer—
Teenage mom, leader of MOPS (Mothers of Preschoolers), and successful author of *Life Interrupted*, *Night Song*, and *From Dust and Ashes*

There are potential pitfalls on the journey to every dream. Try to anticipate what some of these may be for you. Talk to those who have accomplished similar goals and triumphed over adversity. Glean from the wisdom they have to offer.

When anxiety was great within me,
your consolation brought joy to my soul.

Psalm 94:19

You Have a Purpose

"WITH GOD, NOBODY'S HOPELESS."

—FRANKLIN GRAHAM—

SON OF A FAMOUS PREACHER, ONCE A REBELLIOUS SON, NOW A LEADER OF THE
CHARITABLE ORGANIZATION, SAMARITAN'S PURSE, THAT PROVIDES HELP TO
PEOPLE ALL OVER THE GLOBE WHO HAVE BEEN VICTIMS OF EARTHQUAKES,
FLOODS, HURRICANES, AND OTHER NATURAL DISASTERS.

Do you struggle with your identity and wonder what your purpose is in life? Call out to God. He has a specific plan for you, something that no other person can do quite like you. Seek Him first. He will guide you.

"I know the plans I have for you," declares the LORD,
"plans to prosper you and not to harm you,
plans to give you hope and a future."

JEREMIAH 29:11

Dirty Laundry

(Hangin' It Out to Dry)

*You don't have to hang it all out to dry—
put that hot air to good use!*

▸ **GET RID OF STATIC CLING WITH A FABRIC SOFTENER SHEET IN THE DRYER:**

To save a little cash, tear your dryer sheets in half!

▸ **GIVE YOUR CLOTHES A COUPLE SHAKES BEFORE YOU TOSS THEM IN THE DRYER:**

It helps the wrinkles come out in the dryer.

► WATCH YOUR LABELS:

Using the dryer on some clothes means your dog will have a new outfit.

► DRY SWEATERS FLAT INSTEAD OF ON A HANGER:

No one likes shoulder warts!

► TO AVOID SHRINKING YOUR JEANS, HANG THEM TO DRY:

They last longer too.

► OKAY, SO YOU LEFT YOUR CLOTHES IN THE DRYER AND YOU'RE LOOKING AT A BIG WAD OF WRINKLES:

Quick tip: Toss in a damp washcloth and a fresh softener sheet, wait about 3 to 5 minutes, and presto, a wrinkle free outfit!

Don't Take a Step Back with a Setback

"IT'S AMAZING HOW FIRED UP YOU CAN BECOME ROOTING FOR SOMEONE YOU'VE NEVER MET OR HEARD OF BEFORE ... SPORTSMANSHIP AND PASSION ARE OFTEN AT THE FOREFRONT OF EVERY ATHLETE'S PERFORMANCE."

—TYLER HAMILTON—
1991 INJURED WORLD-CLASS SKIER AND 2004 OLYMPIC GOLD MEDAL WINNER IN CYCLING

In the course of our journey, we can slip and fall, but we don't have to stay there. If you've had a setback, remember it is only temporary. God may even have a new direction for you to go. Dust yourself off today and try, try again.

Though a righteous man falls seven times, he rises again, but the wicked are brought down by calamity.

PROVERBS 24:16

Forget the Past

"NEVER GIVE UP!"

—PAUL HAMM—
FROM 12TH PLACE TO 1ST PLACE, FIRST AMERICAN MALE TO WIN
OLYMPIC GOLD ALL AROUND MEN'S GYMNASTICS AND FIRST AMERICAN
EVER TO WIN THREE OLYMPIC MEDALS IN MEN'S GYMNASTICS

You may have lost the round, but you haven't lost the fight. Instead of allowing your failures to pull you down or cause you to focus on the past, determine today to forget those things that are behind you. Set your eyes firmly on your goal and forge on.

Forgetting what is behind and straining toward what is ahead, I press on toward the goal to win the prize for which God has called me heavenward in Christ Jesus.

PHILIPPIANS 3:13-14

Study Much?

*When there is no one to make you study,
you've got to take the initiative on your own.
The best way is to set a goal for yourself. It may
be a certain grade, grade point average, hourly
goal, or even a career goal. Good grades mean
a chance at a better job and a better life.*

▸ STUDY A LITTLE EACH DAY:

Don't wait until test time to cram. Too much pressure
and too little sleep both work against you. Highlight the
main points of what you need to remember.

▸ REVIEW YOUR PREVIOUS STUDY NOTES:

A few days before the test, start reviewing your daily
study notes, especially the highlights. It will help you
to remember everything you've learned so far with
greater accuracy.

▶ **STUDY WITH A GROUP OR PARTNER:**

Study groups bring to light things you may not see on your own and keep you motivated to study longer. Plus it makes studying more fun!

▶ **GET IN A HABIT:**

Humans are creatures of habit. Find a time and place to study on a regular basis. After just a few days, it will become a habit for you and it will become easier and easier to keep that study time.

▶ **KEEP IT QUIET:**

Find a study place with few distractions—the library, dorm lobby, your room, coffee shop, the park. All of those places may be busy places at certain times, but you can find an hour when your roommate is in class or a secluded corner of the lobby where you won't be disturbed.

Walk by Faith

"AS MY VOCATION CONTINUES TO UNFOLD,
I RETURN AGAIN AND AGAIN TO A FUNDAMENTAL
DRIVE TO CREATE AND COMPOSE MUSIC IN
RESPONSE TO THE LARGER WORLD AROUND ME
AND THE PRESENCE OF GOD WITHIN IT."

—JOHN HARVEY—

LEGALLY BLIND IN ONE EYE AND A MULTIMEDIA SPECIALIST, WEB DEVELOPER,
AND RESEARCH ASSISTANT HOLDING A BACHELOR'S AND A MASTER'S DEGREE
IN MUSIC COMPOSITION AND A MASTER'S DEGREE IN MUSIC THEORY.

Do you have a strong sense of
God's hand in your areas of
giftedness? Begin to thank Him
for your talents and make them
a blessing to others.

We live by faith, not by sight.

2 CORINTHIANS 5:7

Think Positive

"IF YOU CANNOT DO GREAT THINGS,
DO SMALL THINGS IN A GREAT WAY."

—NAPOLEON HILL—
SUCCESSFUL BUSINESSMAN AND AUTHOR OF
THE 25 MILLION SOLD, *THE LAW OF SUCCESS*.

Positive thinking generates energy and optimism. Refuse to dwell on the negative aspects of your life. Instead, make a list of your unique gifts and attributes and write down all of the positive aspects of your dream. Think on these things.

Whatever is noble, whatever is right, whatever is pure, whatever is lovely, whatever is admirable—if anything is excellent or praiseworthy—think about such things.

PHILIPPIANS 4:8

MAKE THE
MOMENTS COUNT.

What's Most Important in Life?

There are many things in life that can compete for your attention. When you remind yourself where your priorities are, then it's much easier to make wise decisions.

▶ **GOD:**

Your personal relationship.

▶ **FAMILY:**

They will be yours forever. Care for them. Stay in touch with them.

▶ **YOU:**

Stay healthy in your body and in your mind. Don't neglect yourself or you will be ineffective in your own life and for others.

▶ FRIENDS:

Good friendships take time. Invest in the ones that you want to keep forever.

▶ CAREER:

Your education will take you there—it's your future.

▶ CHURCH:

You will need the support and prayers of your church family.

▶ CHARITY:

The greatest joy in life is giving to others.

▶ FUN:

All work and no play makes you a stressed out, dull person! Save some time to play hard.

▶ REST:

Time for renewal is essential.

"MOTIVATION IS THE SINGLE MOST IMPORTANT
FACTOR IN ANY SORT OF SUCCESS."

—EDMUND HILLARY—
ONE OF THE FIRST MEN TO REACH THE TOP OF MOUNT EVEREST

Write a plan for the
accomplishing of your dream.
List the "supplies" and the
"equipment" that you will need.

*We wait in hope for the LORD;
he is our help and our shield.*

PSALM 33:20

Perseverance

"PEOPLE'S WILDEST DREAMS REACH REALLY FAR. BUT I CERTAINLY NEVER EXPECTED THIS."

—LAURA HILLENBRAND—

AUTHOR OF *SEABISCUIT: AN AMERICAN LEGEND* WHICH HAS SOLD MORE THAN TWO MILLION COPIES AND BECOME A MAJOR MOTION PICTURE. *SEABISCUIT* TOOK FOURTEEN YEARS TO WRITE AS HILLENBRAND WAS SUFFERING FROM CHRONIC FATIGUE SYNDROME, A DEBILITATING, INCURABLE DISEASE.

Don't discount the validity of your dreams or be discouraged at how long it is taking for it to be fulfilled. You will most likely have to work hard while you wait, but the reward will be greater than your imaginings.

Let us throw off everything that hinders ...
and let us run with perseverance the race
marked out for us. Let us fix our eyes on Jesus,
the author and perfecter of our faith.

HEBREWS 12:1-2

Juggling Multiple Priorities

Life has so much to offer, it's easy to overload your schedule and in turn be overwhelmed. But when you prioritize your time and evaluate your activities, you can still accomplish great things and enjoy yourself too!

▶ ASK GOD:

Pray and ask God to give you wisdom regarding your time. The Scriptures say in Proverbs that when you acknowledge God, He will direct your path.

▶ LEARN TO SAY "NO":

You can't do everything that everyone asks of you. And just because there is a need, does not mean you have to fill it. Determine if the task lines up with your goals.

Then determine if you can do it with excellence without compromising your other commitments.

▶ FOLLOW PEACE:

Never commit to something that you feel uneasy about. If you do feel uncomfortable, step back and take time to think it through. Then only commit, once you feel confident in your decision.

▶ COUNT THE COST:

Take into consideration everything it will take, before you dive in, whether it's grad school or a vacation. What does it cost? How much time will it take? Are you excited about it? Do you have the will to follow it through to the end?

▶ IS IT UNETHICAL:

Then the answer is already, "no." Don't even consider it.

Possibilities

"LORD, WHEREVER YOU WANT
ME TO GO, I WILL GO."

—BENSON IDAHOSA—

BORN IN POVERTY AND REJECTED BY HIS FATHER, IDAHOSA
BECAME A GREAT EVANGELIST AND ESTABLISHED MORE THAN
SIX THOUSAND CHURCHES IN NIGERIA AND GHANA AS WELL AS A
BIBLE SCHOOL, TELEVISION MINISTRY, AND MEDICAL CENTER.

What do you believe God has called
you to do? Find promises in His Word
that pertain to the vision He has given
you and write them down. Post the
promises where you will see
them often and dare to believe that
He will do what He says He will do.

*Jesus looked at them and said, "With man this is
impossible, but with God all things are possible."*

MATTHEW 19:26

Make a Difference

"THE WAY YOU OVERCOME SHYNESS IS
TO BECOME SO WRAPPED UP IN SOMETHING
THAT YOU FORGET TO BE AFRAID."

—CLAUDIA ALTA "LADY BIRD" JOHNSON—
FORMER FIRST LADY WHOSE WORK LED TO THE
HIGHWAY BEAUTIFICATION ACT OF 1965

Beautify your world. Plant a rose bush, a tree, or flower. Pick up litter, or remove an eyesore from the landscape. As you pursue the dream in your heart, leave the world around you more beautiful than you found it. Make a difference.

Just tell me what to do and I will do it, Lord.
As long as I live I'll wholeheartedly obey.
Make me walk along the right paths for
I know how delightful they really are.

PSALM 119:33-35 TLB

Staying Safe

Your life is precious and it's okay to take a few precautions to keep yourself safe.

▶ **LOCK YOUR DOORS:**

Whether it's your room, your house, or your car. Keep yourself and your possessions safe. And if you're on the first floor, don't sleep with an open window. Opportunists always look for the easy way to take or break in.

▶ **AFTER DARK, GO AS A TEAM:**

Find a friend to go with if you are heading out after dark. If you must go and no one is around, then let someone know where you're going and when you're returning. Take your cell phone, make sure it's charged up and keep it on.

▶ **EXERCISE WITH A FRIEND:**

If you are exercising outdoors, then do it with a friend. It's safer and it's more fun. If you can't, then make sure you stay in a well traveled area with lots of people around. Bring your cell phone.

► WALK WITH CONFIDENCE:

Thieves look for those who are unprepared. Be observant. Take in what's happening in your surroundings. Be strong and confident in where you are going. If you are heading for your car, have your keys out.

► TAKE A SELF-DEFENSE CLASS:

It's great exercise and a confidence builder. It will help you be prepared for the unexpected.

► KEEP A FLASHLIGHT:

It's good to have one in your car and in your house. If you're ever stranded or without power, you'll want to have easy access to light.

► OWN A SELF-DEFENSE AID:

Stun guns, pepper spray, mace, and other self-defense aids are available. Pick up the one you feel most comfortable with and keep it where you can access it quickly.

► LISTEN TO YOUR CONSCIENCE:

If you feel uneasy about a situation, don't ignore it. The Scriptures tell us that God speaks to our inner man. Take action if something doesn't feel right on the inside.

"MUSIC IS POWERFUL. IT COMMUNICATES THINGS
THAT WORDS CANNOT EXPRESS."

—PHIL KEAGGY—
GIFTED GUITARIST AND POPULAR MUSICIAN

It's never too late to begin
developing your gifts.
Start today. Do something
to train in the talents that
you've already recognized.

*We have different gifts, according
to the grace given us.*

ROMANS 12:6

Step Out

Are you stumbling around in the dark, struggling to find your way? God has sent the Holy Spirit to be your personal mentor, guide, and helper. He may use a variety of things—such as His Word, a pastor, a book, a friend—to point you in the right direction. Simply ask Him, then be open to the possibilities of what He wants you to say and do.

The Comforter (Counselor, Helper, Intercessor, Advocate, Strengthener, Standby), the Holy Spirit, Whom the Father will send in My name [in My place, to represent Me and act on My behalf]. He will teach you all things.

JOHN 14:26 AMP

Staying Grounded in God's Word

*The Bible is God's written Word given to man.
Even though it was written thousands of years
ago, its principles are applicable for today.
It is God's handbook for living a great life.
If you will commit to read the Scriptures on
a regular basis, you will be a better person
and your life will change for the best.*

▶ COMMIT TO READ:

Consistency and quality are better than quantity.
Determine to read a little every day.

▶ WHERE TO START:

Begin with the book of John in the New Testament. Read
some in the Psalms and Proverbs in the Old Testament.
You may want to purchase a one-year Bible that gives

you daily readings for each day of the year. Don't feel guilty if you miss a day, just start in again the next.

▸ Scriptures to Stand On:

Find scriptures that apply to what you are going through. If you need encouragement, peace, strength, healing, money—the Bible has a Word for every area. Bible promise books are great for finding Scriptures according to topics.

▸ Memorize What Means the Most:

When you find a Scripture that helps you, take time to memorize it. If you come up against a problem again, you'll have that verse inside of you. It will help you to stand in faith for the problem to be resolved.

▸ Share the Word:

Find a friend you can share important Scriptures with. If you don't have one, ask God to send one across your path.

Take Off the Limits

"No limit can be placed on what
can be achieved when you accept
God as your partner."

—R. G. LeTourneau—

Genius millionaire engineer responsible for building and
manufacturing large machines including the bulldozer,
road graders, tree crushers, road-building equipment, and
bridge-building equipment. When his company was young and
struggling, he decided to give 90 percent of his income
to God and keep 10 percent. He was soon a millionaire.

Commit yourself to benefit others
with the work you do. Consider the
ideas God has planted in you and
how they might become realities
through your efforts.

*[Jesus said, "God] will give you all you need from
day to day if you live for him and make the
Kingdom of God your primary concern."*

MATTHEW 6:33 NLT

For Wisdom

"I HAVE BEEN DRIVEN MANY TIMES UPON
MY KNEES BY THE OVERWHELMING CONVICTION
THAT I HAD NOWHERE ELSE TO GO."

—ABRAHAM LINCOLN—
PRESIDENT OF THE UNITED STATES OF AMERICA DURING THE CIVIL WAR

Start a prayer journal writing down
everything you pray for and then go
back and record the answers to your
prayers. In times of despair, read over
your answered prayers and see the
handiwork of God in your life.

*To him who is able to do immeasurably more
than all we ask or imaging, according to his power
that is at work within us, to him be glory in the church
and in Christ Jesus throughout all generations,
for ever and ever! Amen.*

EPHESIANS 3:20-21

MAKE THE MOMENTS COUNT.

Win Favor with Teachers and Supervisors

There are some simple things you can do to help you succeed in school as well as the working world. It's amazing how many people will not do these seemingly obvious things and they can make such a difference.

▶ BE EARLY AND STAY LATE:

Get to class, work, or meetings 5 or 10 minutes early and stay a little late. It shows your commitment to learn and do everything you can to succeed.

▶ TURN ASSIGNMENTS IN EARLY:

Whether it's a week or even 20 minutes. It shows your teachers and/or supervisors that they can depend on you.

► Talk Less, Listen More:

Avoid putting your foot in your mouth by first thinking your response through. It's not about who gets to dominate the conversation, it's about who has the best input.

► Be Grateful:

Showing respect and honor to your teachers or supervisors is important and Biblical. Say "thank-you" with sincerity and often. Make your requests by saying "please." Never assume someone else's responsibility. Make sure you ask first.

► Go the Extra Mile:

When you can, do more than is requested. Teachers and managers are thrilled when they receive more than they expected.

Training

"I LOVE COMPETING. I WANT TO SUCCEED."

—TARA LIPINSKI—
WORLD FIGURE SKATING CHAMPION AND OLYMPIC GOLD MEDALIST

Do you have a dream of succeeding? Submit yourself to a time of training. Listen and follow the directions of your instructor as closely as you are able. Discipline yourself to work hard even if you don't feel like it. The rewards will be worth it all.

Take hold of instruction; do not let go.
Guard her, for she is your life.

PROVERBS 4:13 NASB

Turned for Good

"EACH STRUGGLE, EACH DEFEAT, SHARPENS YOUR
SKILLS AND STRENGTHS, YOUR COURAGE AND YOUR
ENDURANCE, YOUR ABILITY AND YOUR CONFIDENCE
AND THUS EACH OBSTACLE IS A COMRADE-IN-ARMS
FORCING YOU TO BECOME BETTER ... OR QUIT."

—OG MANDINO—
BESTSELLING AUTHOR OF *THE GREATEST SALESMAN IN THE WORLD*
AND MANY OTHER LIFE-INSPIRING NOVELS.

When you pray and **seek God** for
answers to your struggles, He can
work those negative aspects of your
life for your benefit. If you are
discouraged about the course of
your life, take some time to pray and
read God's Word.

We know that all things work together for
good to them that love God, to them who
are the called according to his purpose.

ROMANS 8:28 KJV

How to Complete a Project

Whether you are working alone or with a team to get a project done, a few simple steps can help you get it done on time.

▶ **MAKE A STEP-BY-STEP PLAN:**

Write it down. Don't try to figure everything out in your head. When you put it on paper, you're able to think through each step.

▶ **DELEGATE:**

If you can. Let other people help you. Even if it seems easier to do it all yourself, bringing others in can take pressure off of you and may actually get results that are better than if you did it alone.

▸ Set Due Dates:

Be reasonable about it and give each step enough time to be done with excellence.

▸ Plan a Reward:

When you are finished, have something special for each person helping or for yourself if you are completing the project alone.

▸ Inspect What You Expect:

When others are helping you, make sure you check out their work. Fine-tuning might be needed in the process so that you're not unpleasantly surprised at the end, or end up doing the project over yourself.

"PIONEERS HAVE LONELY JOURNEYS,
AND THEY'RE BREAKING BARRIERS AND MYTHS
THAT OTHER PEOPLE HAVE NOT TREAD UPON."

—MADELINE MANNING MIMS—
AFRICAN-AMERICAN ATHLETE, FOUR-TIME OLYMPIAN,
ORDAINED MINISTER, AND MOTIVATIONAL SPEAKER

What barriers are
holding you back?
Can you step up and
break them down?

By faith the walls of Jericho fell.

HEBREWS 11:30

Start Somewhere

"Never lose an opportunity to use a practical beginning, however small, for it is wonderful how often in such matters the mustard seed germinates and roots itself."

—Florence Nightingale—
Superintendent of a London hospital who revolutionized the field of nursing during the Crimean War. Her findings on sanitation, including simple hand washing, reformed infection control.

When you have a dream, you have to start somewhere with it. No matter how small it may seem at the time, start anyway. As you are faithful in the small things, you will eventually move into areas greater than you could have imagined!

[Jesus said,] "I tell you the truth, if you have faith as small as a mustard seed, you can say to this mountain 'Move from here to there' and it will move. Nothing will be impossible for you."

Matthew 17:20

Finding a Good Church Home

*When you are out on your own, it's important
to have a faith family who supports you in
prayer and encourages you in your faith.
No church is perfect, but here are some
things to look for in a good church.*

▶ ENCOURAGEMENT IN THE SCRIPTURES:

Look for a church that teaches from the Scripture. You should be learning and growing each time you go to church. If you don't feel any different when you leave, it may not be the right church for you.

▶ WORSHIP:

A good church should lead you into praise and worship. Churches have different styles—some traditional, some contemporary. Look for a worship time that you can enter into and lift your heart and praises to God.

► FRIENDLY:

A good church should make you feel welcome. That doesn't mean everyone instantly becomes your best friend because all relationships take time. But there should be a warm environment with people who are full of God's love.

► MEETS YOUR SPIRITUAL NEEDS:

The church that is right for you should be able to meet your needs. Check out their small groups or Sunday school classes. Look for a place where you feel a sense of belonging in the church.

► OUTREACH:

A church led by the Spirit of God should have some form of outreach. Small churches may not be able to do as much, but all churches should have a way to reach out to their community and the world.

References

Unless otherwise marked, Scripture quotations are taken from the *Holy Bible: New International Version,* (North American Edition)®. Copyright 1973, 1978, 1984 by International Bible Society. Used by permission of Zondervan Publishing House. All rights reserved.

Scripture quotations marked KJV are taken from *The King James Version* of the Bible.

Scripture quotations marked NKJV are taken from *The Holy Bible, New King James Version.* Copyright © 1982 by Thomas Nelson, Inc. Used by permission.

Scripture quotations marked THE MESSAGE are taken from *The Message.* Copyright © 1993, 1994, 1995, 1996. Used by permission of NavPress Publishing Group.

Scripture quotations marked NASB are taken from the *New American Standard Bible*®. Copyright © 1960, 1962, 1963, 1968, 1971, 1972, 1973, 1975, 1977, 1995 by The Lockman Foundation. Used by permission.

Scripture quotations marked TLB are taken from *The Holy Bible, The Living Bible Translation.* Copyright © 1971. Used by permission of Tyndale House Publishers, Inc., Wheaton, Illinois 60189. All rights reserved.

Scripture quotations marked NLT are taken from *The Holy Bible, New Living Translation.* Copyright © 1996. Used by permission of Tyndale House Publishers, Inc., Wheaton, Illinois 60189. All right reserved.

This and other titles by White Stone Books are available from your local bookstore.

If you enjoyed this we would love to hear from you.

Visit our Web site at:
www.whitestonebooks.com

*"... To him who overcomes I will give
some of the hidden manna to eat.
And I will give him a white stone, and on
the stone a new name written which no one
knows except him who receives it."*

REVELATION 2:17 NKJV

WHITE STONE BOOKS
LAKELAND, FLORIDA